Python

Programming Basics
for Absolute Beginners

Nathan Clark

Books in this Series

Computer Programming for Beginners

Fundamentals of Programming Terms and Concepts

PYTHON

Programming Basics for Absolute Beginners

Table of Contents

Introduction --- 1

1. What is Python? -- 3

2. History of Python -- 7

3. Features of Python -- 11

4. Building Your Environment--------------------------------------- 15

5. Your First Python Program ------------------------------------- 21

6. Data Types --- 29

7. Variables --- 35

8. Operators -- 41

9. Decision Making in Python ------------------------------------- 53

10. Loops --- 59

11. Working with Numbers--- 67

12. Working with Strings -- 75

13. Type Conversion --- 89

Conclusion -- 93

Introduction

Welcome to the wonderful world of programming, the chapters contained in this book will give you a basic understanding of programming in Python. By its final chapter you will be able to create a complete program on your own, using Python.

This guide is aimed at newcomers to Python. If however you are completely new to programming, I recommend first reading our primer to programming. It covers all the concepts, terms, programming paradigms and coding techniques that a complete novice needs to know.

Computer Programming for Beginners

Fundamentals of Programming Terms and Concepts

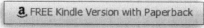

An important aspect of this series, and your learning experience, is **learning by doing**. Practical examples are proven to be the best way to learn a programming language, which is why I have crammed as many examples into this guide as possible. I have tried to keep the core of the examples similar, so the only variable is the topic under discussion. This makes it easier to understand what we are implementing. As you progress through the chapters, remember to follow along with the examples and try them yourself.

In order to use the information contained in this book, you must have a computer that runs Windows, Macintosh, Linux, or UNIX operating system. You must know how to run a program, copy a file, create a folder, and navigate through menus. These are the only requirements for being able to program using Python.

Thank you for your interest in this versatile language and let's have some fun!

1. What is Python?

Python is a high-level programming language that was first released in 1991. It is a powerful language that is used widely across the world today. The initial intent of this programming language was to allow programmers to convert requirements to code using less lines of code. This is something that is very noticeable if you are familiar with other programming languages.

This language is currently used by a number of large companies, such as YouTube, for building the backend of web programs. It is also used extensively in the areas of data science and data analytics. As mentioned, one of the biggest selling points of Python is the simplicity of its programs. It's not necessary to write an enormous amount of code to get a working program.

A sample Python program is shown below.

Example 1: The following program shows how to add 2 numbers in Python.

```
i=3
j=2
print('The sum of the numbers is')
print(i+j)
```

From the above example we can see how simple it is to write Python code. During the course of this book you will learn how to write programs such as the one above, as well as more advanced concepts that will enable you to write complete application programs.

Before we get into writing your very first program, let's look at some of the design goals of Python.

1.1 Intended for Smaller Programs

If you compare Python with another popular programming language like Java, you will notice that the number of lines of code for an equivalent program will be around 3-5 times shorter. One of the primary reasons for this, when you look at the above code sample, is not having the need to define the data type for variables.

In Java, if we need to have a variable defined, we would need to ensure that the variable was declared with an associated data type as shown below. Here, the keyword 'int' declares the variable as an integer number.

```
int i;
i=5;
```

So in Java, and most other programming languages, we have to first indicate that the variable will be of a certain data type and then assign the value to it. However in python, we simply assign the chosen value to the variable, as shown below.

```
i=5
```

That's it. We have saved time in declaring the variable, because of Python's built-in high-level data types and its dynamic typing feature.

1.2 Interactivity

Python has an interactive shell that allows you to easily start working with code. An example screenshot is shown below. So after Python is installed, you can immediately start issuing statements without the need for additional installations.

```
Command Prompt - python

C:\Users\techuser>python
Python 3.6.3 (v3.6.3:2c5fed8, Oct  3 2017, 17:26:49) [MSC v.1900 32 bit (Intel)] on win32
Type "help", "copyright", "credits" or "license" for more information.
>>> 2+3
5
>>>
```

1.3 Object Oriented

Object oriented programming is a feature that is available in most programming languages. This paradigm is based on the concept of using objects in order to represent everyday aspects. We could, for instance, have an 'Employee' class, with attributes for a 'Name' and 'ID'.

A sample Python program is shown below that defines such a class.

Example 2: The following program shows how to define a class in Python.

```
class Employee:
   def displayCount(self):
```

```
    print("This is an employee class")
emp1 = Employee()
emp1.displayCount()
```

1.4 Extensive and Rich Library

One of the biggest advantages of Python is its rich set of plug-in libraries. These libraries provide numerous common functionalities, which means that developers don't need to write them manually. Just link a library and off you go. The different categories of libraries available are given below.

- Graphical user interfaces

- Web frameworks

- Multimedia

- Databases

- Networking

- Test frameworks

- Automation

- Web scraping

- Documentation

- System administration

- Scientific computing

- Text processing

- Image processing

2. History of Python

The Python language was designed by Guido van Rossum and first appeared on the scene in 1991. The most significant changes to the language were made in the year 2000 when Python version 2.0 was released. There are currently two stable releases for Python, that being Python 3.6 and 2.7.

Below is a summary of Python's release history.

Version	Release Date
0.9.0	February 20, 1991
2.0	October 16, 2000
2.1	April 17, 2001
2.2	December 21, 2001
2.3	July 29, 2003
2.4	November 30, 2004
2.5	September 16, 2006
3.0	December 3, 2008

Let's look at some of the features introduced for Python 2.7:

- Numeric handling has been improved in many ways, for both floating-point numbers and for the 'Decimal' class.

- Sets are built into Python as lists and dictionaries.

- The 'assertRaises' module now works as a context manager.

- A C-optimized I/O package for better input/output management.

- Inclusion of the 'OrderedDict' API, which provides the same interface as regular dictionaries but iterates over keys and values in a guaranteed order depending on when a key was first inserted.

- The 'argparse' module for parsing command line arguments was added as a more powerful replacement to the 'optparse' module.

- A 'dictConfig' function was added that uses a dictionary to configure logging.

The newest release of Python 3.6 introduced the following features:

- The 'asyncio' module received new features, significant usability and performance improvements, and a fair amount of bug fixes.

- A new file system path protocol has been implemented to support path-like objects. All standard library functions operating on paths have been updated to work with the new protocol.

- The new 'secrets' module was added to simplify the generation of cryptographically strong pseudo-random numbers, suitable for managing confidential aspects such as account authentication and tokens.

- The ability to use underscores in numeric literals was added, for improved readability.

- Added support for using 'async' in list, set and dict comprehensions.

- The default console in Windows now accepts all Unicode characters, and provides correctly read 'str' objects to Python code.

3. Features of Python

Python has many programming features that make it a great choice as a programming language. Let's look at a few of them next.

3.1 Operator Support

Python supports the basic operations such as Arithmetic Operators, Comparison (Relational) Operators, Assignment Operators, Logical Operators, Bitwise Operators, Membership Operators, and Identity Operators. An example of using operators in Python is given below.

Example 3: The next program showcases the use of operators in Python.

```
i=4
if ( i < 5 ):
   print("The value of i is less than 5")
```

3.2 Decision Making Statements

Python has the ability to work with decision making statements, such as 'if' statements and 'if else' statements. This allows the program to execute a specified block of code, based on the outcome of a condition. An example of a decision making statement in Python is given below.

Example 4: The following program shows how to use decision making statements in Python.

```
i=4
if ( i < 5 ):
   print("The value of i is less than 5")
```

3.3 Iterative Loop Statements

Python also has the ability to run blocks of code multiple times by using iterative statements. These statements loop a specified block of code multiple times based on the outcome of a condition. An example of an iterative statement in Python is given below.

Example 5: The following program showcases the use of iterative statements in Python.

```
#!/usr/bin/python
count = 0
while (count < 5):
   print('The count is:', count)
   count = count + 1
```

3.4 Ability to Use Lists

Python has the ability to use a sequence of values known as lists. A list is an array that can store multiple pieces of information, which can then be referenced individually at a later point in time. An example of lists in Python is given below.

Example 6: The following program showcases the use of lists in Python.

```
list1 = [1, 2, 3, 4, 5 ];
print(list1[0:5])
```

3.5 Ability to Use Functions

It is always important to use functions to break large sections of code into smaller logical chunks that can be managed separately. When using functions you can also pass values, which is an integral part of all programs. An example of a function in Python is given below.

Example 7: The following program showcases the use of functions in Python.

```
def code():
    print("This is a sample function")
code()
```

3.6 Ability to Take Input

Python has the ability to create programs than can take input from the user and then display that input accordingly. This allows for greater functionality on the user end of the program. An example of input functionality in Python is given below.

Example 8: The following program shows how to take input from the user in Python.

```
#!/usr/bin/python
```

```
str = input("Enter what needs to be displayed ")
print("The displayed result is : ", str)
```

3.7 Working with Classes and Objects

As we discussed earlier, Python is an object oriented language. And as with all object oriented languages, Python has the support for classes and objects. An example of a class definition in Python is given below.

Example 9: The following program shows how to define a class in Python.

```
class Employee:
   def displayCount(self):
     print("This is an employee class")
emp1 = Employee()
emp1.displayCount()
```

4. Building Your Environment

In order to start working with Python, there are various options available. The first order of business is to ensure that the Python Runtime is installed on your system. The various versions of Python can be downloaded from the following link:

https://www.python.org/downloads/

Currently, at the time of writing this book, there are two main stable releases for Python that are preferred by developers. Those are Python 3.6 and Python 2.7. Python can be downloaded for Windows, Linux and MacOS, and you are also welcome to download any other release version of Python.

Some key points to note here are:

- All Python releases are open-source.

- For most Unix systems, you must download and compile the source code. The same source code archive can be used to build the Windows and Mac versions, and is the starting point for ports to all other platforms.

Once you have Python installed, you can immediately start working with the Python terminal and execute commands. If you invoke Python in Windows, the terminal should look like the sample screenshot below.

```
Command Prompt - python
Microsoft Windows [Version 10.0.16299.248]
(c) 2017 Microsoft Corporation. All rights reserved.

C:\Users\techuser>python
Python 3.6.3 (v3.6.3:2c5fed8, Oct  3 2017, 17:26:49) [MSC v.1900 32 bit (Intel)] on win32
Type "help", "copyright", "credits" or "license" for more information.
>>> print("You are now working on Python")
You are now working on Python
>>> _
```

4.1 Using Other Editors

If you don't want to use a simple text editor, you can also use one of many Integrated Development Environments (IDE's) available that can run Python. An IDE makes programming much easier by aiding in the development process. Some of the most popular editors with their common features are given below.

Python for Visual Studio Code

Some of the core features of the tool are:

- Integrated Development Environment features, such as automatic indenting, code navigation and rename factoring.

- IntelliSense and autocomplete.

- Code formatting.

- Support for multiple linters with custom settings.

- Ability for debugging by using the following tools: watch window, evaluate expressions, step through code, add/remove breakpoints, local variables, and arguments.

- Support for unit testing by using unittest, pytest, and nose.

Pydev for Eclipse

If you have worked with Java, you would probably be familiar with Eclipse. Eclipse has a specific plugin available for Python, called Pydev. Some of the core features of the tool are:

- Code completion.

- Ability to perform code analysis.

- Availability of a debugger and remote debugger.

- A debug console that allows for interactive probing in suspended mode.

- Support for Python 2.x and 3.x syntax.

- Ability to show parser errors.

PyCharm by Jetbrains

While the two IDE's mentioned above are free, PyCharm is a commercially available IDE. Some of the core features of the tool are:

- Better code quality - PyCharm helps to keep code quality under control with PEP8 checks, testing assistance, and a host of inspections.

- Safe refactoring - Refactoring is done via safe renaming and delete, extracting methods, introducing variables, inline variables or methods, and language and framework-specific refactoring.

- Availability of other tools - PyCharm has a large collection of tools out of the box such as an integrated debugger and test runner, Python profiler, a built-in terminal, remote development capabilities, an integrated SSH terminal, and integration with Docker and Vagrant.

- Ability to access databases - PyCharm can access Oracle, SQL Server, PostgreSQL, MySQL and other databases right from the IDE.

Below is an example of how an IDE looks. This specific IDE is Visual Studio Code.

4.2 Other tools

Some of the other tools that can also be useful during the Python development process are given below. Remember these tools are also optional but, like IDE's, can make programming a better experience.

Pylint

Pylint is a Python source code analyzer that looks for programming errors and helps to enforce a coding standard. Different rules are defined that are used to detect problems in the code, and the code is then checked against these rules. Below is a link to the Pylint tool.

https://pypi.org/project/pylint/

Pytest

This framework allows you to create test cases in order to test your Python code. It's vital to test code to ensure that the program runs as intended, before being issued to the end-user. Below is a link to the Pytest framework.

https://docs.pytest.org/en/latest/

5. Your First Python Program

We have seen how to get the environment set up, to be able to code in Python. In this chapter we'll focus on writing our very own Python programs. In a previous chapter, we had a sneak peek at how to execute Python statements in the interpreter. Below is a snapshot of the Python interpreter, where we write the following command:

```
print("Hello World")
```

The 'print' command is used to output text back to the console. In the remainder of this book, we will focus on writing programs that can encapsulate these code statements in order to build bigger and better programs in Python.

Creating a Python File

We start by creating a new file. We can either use an Integrated Development Environment, or simply create a file in Notepad. We will do the latter, seeing as it's much easier as a beginner.

Let's look at the steps to create a simple Python program:

- Create a new file in Notepad.

- Add the following line of code inside the file.

```
print("Hello World")
```

- Save the file as 'Demo.py'. Note that we are saving the file with the .py extension. This helps ensure that the Python runtime will be able to interpret the file and run it accordingly.

Running a Python File

Next, depending on the environment you are in, there are different ways to run the program. In Windows we can carry out the following steps:

- Open Windows PowerShell by using the Windows search feature.

- In PowerShell, type the following command.

```
& python 'location of the file'
```

In the screenshot below, our Python code file is located on H drive.

```
Administrator: Windows PowerShell
Windows PowerShell
Copyright (C) Microsoft Corporation. All rights reserved.

PS C:\WINDOWS\system32> & python H:/Demo.py
Hello World
PS C:\WINDOWS\system32> _
```

- When we hit enter, we get the relevant output 'Hello World'. That's it!

What happens in the above process is that PowerShell submits our program to the Python interpreter, which then executes the program and returns the output back to the PowerShell console. This simple flow is depicted below.

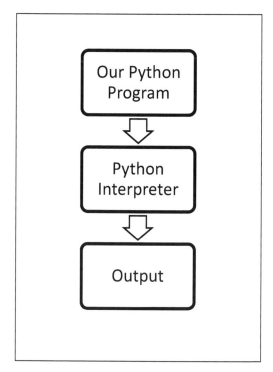

Now let's add a couple more lines of code to see how to execute multiple statements in Python.

Example 10: The following program is used to explore our first Python program further.

In our current program, let's add the following lines:

```
print("This is our first program")
print("We want to write to the console")
print("Hello World")
```

Note that unlike other programming languages, there is no main method or extra code needed to define the entry point for the program. It's just plain and simple code that gets executed.

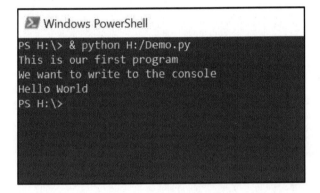

From the output above, we can see that all the lines of code are executed and the relevant text is written to the console.

The Python interpreter does the basic error checking for our Python programs. To illustrate how this works, let's make a mistake in our next program.

Example 11: The following program is used to introduce an error into the program.

Let's change our code to the following:

```
print{"This is our first program"}
print("We want to write to the console")
print("Hello World")
```

Note that we have changed the first line of code and used curly braces instead of the standard brackets. When we execute the program, we will get the following output:

PS H:\\> & python H:/Demo.py

  File "H:/Demo.py", line 1

   print{"This is our first program"}

SyntaxError: invalid syntax

Here we can see that the Python interpreter has checked the correctness of the program and pointed out the error accordingly.

5.1 Defining Values

We can also define values in a Python program. We will be looking at this in more detail in subsequent chapters, but for now let's look at a simple example of how this can be done.

Example 12: The following program shows how we work with values in a program.

```
a="5"
print("The value of a is "+a)
```

This program's output will be as follows:

The value of a is 5

In the above program:

- We first defined a variable called 'a'.

- We then assigned a value of '5' to this variable.

- We also use the 'print' statement to output the value of the variable.

- Note that in the print statement, we added the text 'The value of a is' before the actual value of the variable 'a'.

5.2 Using Python Libraries

Python has a host of built-in libraries that provide additional functionality to Python programs. We will be looking at this in greater detail later on, but for now let's look at a simple example of how this works.

Example 13: The following program shows how to work with Python libraries.

```
print(sum([1,2,3]))
```

This program's output will be as follows:

6

In the above program:

- We are making use of the math library.

- This is a built-in library that is always available.

- We then use the 'sum' method in that library to carry out the multiplication of the numbers.

- Lastly, we print the resultant value to the console.

We can also use other library modules which are not directly accessible. This is done by importing them. Let's look at an example of this.

Example 14: The following program illustrates how to import Python libraries.

```
import random
print(random.randint(1,5))
```

This program's output will depend on what gets generated. In our case we received the following:

3

In the above program:

- We are first using the 'import' statement to get the functionality of the 'random' library.

- We then use the 'randint' method to generate a random number between 1 and 5.

- Lastly we display that value to the console.

5.3 Using Comments

Comments are extremely useful in any programming language to ensure better readability and maintainability of the program. Their main purpose is to describe the various sections of the program for future reference. Let's look at the use of comments in Python.

Example 15: The following program shows how to use comments in a program.

```
# This program generates a random number
import random
print(random.randint(1,5))
```

In this sample program, the first line starts with a '#' which indicates that this is a comment line. As such, this line will not be executed and will be ignored by the interpreter.

6. Data Types

Data types are used to store different types of data. For example, if we wanted to store text data we would use a string data type, and if we wanted to store a number we would use a number or integer data type. Data types also help to reduce errors when defining variables, by assigning a specific data type to a variable.

The available data types depend on the programming language being used. Let's look at the data types available in Python.

Table 1: Data Types

Data Type	Purpose
boolean	Used to define Boolean values of true or false
int	Used to define integers
float	Used to define floating point numbers
complex	Used to define complex numbers
str	Used to define a sequence of characters

Let's go over each data type in more detail with the help of a Python program as an example.

6.1 Boolean Data Type

This data type is used to define Boolean values. Boolean data can only have one of two possible values, True or False. This should not be confused with strings (str) which will be covered in a moment.

Example 16: The following program showcases the Boolean data type.

```
# This program looks at different data types
a=True
print(a)
```

This program's output will be as follows:

True

In the above program:

- We are declaring a variable called 'a'.

- This is assigned a Boolean value of 'True'.

- We are then displaying this value to the console.

We can easily define multiple Boolean values in a program, as shown next.

Example 17: The next program shows how we can use multiple Boolean values.

```
# This program looks at different data types
a=True
b=False
print(a)
print(b)
```

This program's output will be as follows:

True

False

6.2 Int Data Type

This data type is used to define integer number values. An integer is simply a whole number without fractions or decimals.

Example 18: The following program showcases the integer data type.

```
# This program looks at different data types
a=123
b=345
print(a)
print(b)
```

This program's output will be as follows:

123

345

In the above program:

- We are declaring 2 variables called 'a' and 'b'.

- We then assign whole numbers to these variables.

- Lastly, we display the values to the console.

6.3 Float Data Type

This data type is used to define floating point numbers. Floating point numbers are simply numbers that have fractional parts expressed with a decimal point.

Example 19: The following program showcases the float data type.

```
# This program looks at different data types
a=2.23
print(a)
```

This program's output will be as follows:

2.23

In the above program:

- We are declaring a variable called 'a'.

- We then assign a fractional number value to this variable.

- Lastly, we display the value to the console.

6.4 Complex Data Type

This data type is used to define complex numbers. In Python, placing a 'J' or 'j' after a number makes it imaginary, making it possible to write complex literals easily. The 'j' originates from engineering and is used instead of the more common 'i', as found in mathematics and statistics.

Example 20: The following program showcases the complex data type.

```
# This program looks at different data types
a=3.14J
print(a)
```

This program's output will be as follows:

3.14j

In the above program:

- We are declaring a variable called 'a'.

- We then assign a complex number to this variable.

- Lastly, we display the value to the console.

6.5 Str Data Type

This data type is used to define a sequence of characters or, simply put, a text string. The text string is indicated with the use of quotation marks ("").

Example 21: The following program showcases the string data type.

```
# This program looks at different data types
a="Hello World"
print(a)
```

This program's output will be as follows:

Hello World

In the above program:

- We are declaring a variable called 'a'.

- We then assign a string to this variable.

- Lastly, we display the value to the console.

7. Variables

Variables are used to define values based on the various data types we discussed earlier. A variable's main purpose is to be referenced during the course of the program. So instead of writing out a value numerous times, we can just reference the variable. We can also change the value of the variable at any time. Let's look at the different types of variables we can create based on their data type.

7.1 Boolean Variables

These are variables that are used to hold Boolean values, which can be changed at any point in time during the course of the program. Boolean values can only be 'True' or 'False'. Let's look at an example of how they are defined.

Example 22: The following program shows how to use Boolean type variables.

```
# This program looks at different data types
a=True
print(a)
a=False
print(a)
```

This program's output will be as follows:

True
False

In the above program:

- We are first defining a variable called 'a'.

- This holds a Boolean value of 'True'.

- Then we display this value to the console.

- In the next statement we change the value assigned to this variable to 'False'.

- We then display the new value to the console.

7.2 Int Variables

These are variables that are used to hold integer values, which can be changed at any point in time in the program. Recall that integer values are whole numbers, without fractions or decimals. Let's look at an example of how they are defined.

Example 23: This program shows how to use int type variables.

```
# This program looks at different data types
a=1
print(a)
a=2
print(a)
```

This program's output will be as follows:

1

2

In the above program:

- We are first defining a variable called 'a'.

- This holds an integer value of 1.

- We then display this value to the console.

- In the next section, we change the value assigned to this variable to 2.

- We then display the new value to the console.

7.3 Float Variables

These are variables that hold floating point values, which can be changed at any point in time during the course of the program. As mentioned earlier, floating point values are numbers that have fractional parts expressed with a decimal point. Let's look at an example of how they are defined.

Example 24: The following program shows how to use float type variables.

```
# This program looks at different data types
a=1.11
print(a)
a=2.22
print(a)
```

This program's output will be as follows:

1.11

2.22

In the above program:

- We are first defining a variable called 'a'.

- This holds a floating point value of 1.11.

- We then display this value to the console.

- We decide to change the value assigned to this variable to 2.22.

- We then display the new value to the console.

7.4 Complex Variables

These are variables used to hold complex values, which can be changed at any point in time in the program. Recall that complex literals are possible in Python via the use of the 'J' or 'j' suffix. Let's look at an example of how they are defined.

Example 25: The following program showcases the use of complex type variables.

```
# This program looks at different data types
a=1.11J
print(a)
a=2.22J
print(a)
```

This program's output will be as follows:

1.11j

2.22j

In the above program:

- We are first defining a variable called 'a'.

- This holds complex number value of 1.11J.

- We then display this value to the console.

- We decide to change the value assigned to this variable to 2.22J.

- We then display the new value to the console.

7.5 String Variables

These are variables that hold string values, which can be changed at any point during the course of the program. String values are simply text characters. Let's look at an example of how they are defined.

Example 26: The following program shows how to use string type variables.

```
# This program looks at different data types
a="Hello"
print(a)
a="World"
print(a)
```

This program's output will be as follows:

Hello

World

In the above program:

- We are first defining a variable called 'a'.

- This holds a string value of 'Hello'.

- We then display this value to the console.

- In the next section, we change the value assigned to this variable to 'World'.

- We then display the new value to the console.

8. Operators

There are various types of operators available for use in Python. An operator is a symbol that instructs the Python interpreter to perform a specific operation on the defined variables, such as multiplication or a comparison. Let's look at each category of operators in greater detail.

8.1 Arithmetic Operators

These are operators that are used to work with numbers. They perform a mathematical function on two operands and return a numerical value. The most common arithmetic operators are shown below.

Table 2: Arithmetic Operators

Operator	Operation
+	Used to add two operands
-	Used to subtract one operand from another
*	Used to multiply two operands
/	Used to divide one operand by another
%	Gives the remainder value after a division

Example 27: The following program showcases arithmetic operators.

```
# Working with operators
i=10
j=3
print("The addition of the two operands")
print(i+j)
print("The subtraction of the two operands")
print(i-j)
print("The multiplication of the two operands")
print(i*j)
print("The division of the two operands")
print(i/j)
print("The remainder of the two operands")
print(i%j)
```

This program's output will be as follows:

The addition of the two operands
13

The subtraction of the two operands
7

The multiplication of the two operands
30

The division of the two operands
3.3333333333333335

The remainder of the two operands
1

8.2 Relational Operators

These are operators that are used to determine the value of conditions based on the value of the operands. In other words, they are based on the relationship between two operands. The relational operators possible in Python are given below.

Table 3: Relational Operators

Operator	Operation
==	Checks if two operands are equal
!=	Checks if two operands are not equal
>	Checks if one operand is greater than another
<	Checks if one operand is less than another
>=	Checks if one operand is greater than or equal to another
<=	Check if one operand is less than or equal to another

If a condition evaluates to true, then a value of 1 is returned. Else a value of 0 is returned. Let's look at an example of these operators in action.

Example 28: This program shows how we can use relational operators.

```
# Working with operators
i=10
j=3
print("Is i equal to j")
print(i==j)
```

```
print("Is i not equal to j")
print(i!=j)
print("Is i greater than j")
print(i>j)
print("Is i less than j")
print(i<j)
print("Is i greater than or equal j")
print(i>=j)
print("Is i less than or equal j")
print(i<=j)
```

This program's output will be as follows:

Is i equal to j
False

Is i not equal to j
True

Is i greater than j
True

Is i less than j
False

Is i greater than or equal j
True

Is i less than or equal j
False

8.3 Logical Operators

These are operators used to determine the value of conditions based on the value of the operands, where the operands are

Boolean values. Hence these operators work exclusively with True / False values. The logical operators possible in Python are given below.

Table 4: Relational Operators

Operator	Operation
&&	This is the logical AND operator
||	This is the logical OR operator
!	This is the logical NOT operator

Below is a table for the logical AND operator, based on the possible value combinations of the operands. We will also look at an example to illustrate their function.

Table 4.1: Relational Operators - AND

Operand A	Operand B	Result
True	True	1
True	False	0
False	True	0
False	False	0

Example 29: The following program shows how we can use the logical AND operator.

```
# Working with operators
i=True
j=True
```

```
k=False
print("i AND j")
print(i and j)
print("i AND k")
print(i and k)
print("k AND i")
print(k and i)
print("k AND k")
print(k and k)
```

This program's output will be as follows:

i AND j
True

i AND k
False

k AND i
False

k AND k
False

Next is a table for the logical OR operator, based on the possible value combinations of the operands. Again, we will also look at an example to illustrate their function.

Table 4.2: Relational Operators - OR

Operand A	Operand B	Result
True	True	1
True	False	1
False	True	1

Operand A	Operand B	Result
False	False	0

Example 30: The following program shows how we can use the logical OR operator.

```
# Working with operators
i=True
j=True
k=False
print("i OR j")
print(i or j)
print("i OR k")
print(i or k)
print("k OR i")
print(k or i)
print("k OR k")
print(k or k)
```

This program's output will be as follows

i OR j
True

i OR k
True

k OR i
True

k OR k
False

Lastly is a table for the logical NOT operator, based on the two possible values of the operands. We will also look at a simple example to illustrate their function.

Table 4.3: Relational Operators - NOT

Operand A	Result
True	0
False	1

Example 31: The following program shows how we can use the logical NOT operator.

```
# Working with operators
i=True
j=False
print("NOT i")
print(not i)
print("NOT j")
print(not j)
```

This program's output will be as follows:

NOT i
False

NOT j
True

8.4 Assignment Operators

These are operators that are used to make assignment operations easier. An assignment operation is when we assign a value to a variable. Below is a table of the assignment operators possible in Python. All but the first operator combines an arithmetic function with the assignment function.

Table 5: Assignment Operators

Operator	Operation
=	This is used to assign the value of an operation to an operand
+=	This is used to carry out the addition and assignment operator in one go
-=	This is used to carry out the subtraction and assignment operator in one go
*=	This is used to carry out the multiplication and assignment operator in one go
/=	This is used to carry out the division and assignment operator in one go
%=	This is used to carry out the modulus and assignment operator in one go

Now let's look at how we can implement these operators in more detail.

Example 32: The following program shows how to use assignment operators.

```
# Working with operators
i=10
j=3
print("The value of i+=j is")
i += j
print(i)
print("The value of i-=j is")
i -= j
print(i)
print("The value of i*=j is")
i *= j
print(i)
print("The value of i/=j is")
i /= j
print(i)
print("The value of i%=j is")
i %= j
print(i)
```

This program's output will be as follows

The value of i+=j is
13

The value of i-=j is
10

The value of i*=j is
30

The value of i/=j is
10.0

The value of i%=j is

1.0

8.5 Bitwise Operators

These operators are used to make bit operations on operands. They perform an action on the bits of a number when converted to binary. As such they are not commonly used in real life. The bitwise operators possible in Python are given below, with a sample program.

Table 6: Bitwise Operators

Operator	Operation
&	This copies a bit to the result if it exists in both operands
|	This copies a bit to the result if it exists in either operand
^	This copies a bit to the result if it exists in one operand but not in both
<<	Here the left operand value is moved left by the number of bits specified by the right operand
>>	Here the left operand value is moved right by the number of bits specified by the right operand

Example 33: The following program shows how we can use bitwise operators.

```
# Working with operators
i=10
j=3
print("Showcasing the & bit operator")
print(i & j)
print("Showcasing the | bit operator")
print(i | j)
print("Showcasing the ^ bit operator")
print(i ^ j)
print("Showcasing the << bit operator")
print(i << 2)
print("Showcasing the >> bit operator")
print(i >> 2)
```

This program's output will be as follows

Showcasing the & bit operator
2

Showcasing the | bit operator
11

Showcasing the ^ bit operator
9

Showcasing the << bit operator
40

Showcasing the >> bit operator
2

9. Decision Making in Python

Decision making statements will execute code only if a particular condition holds true. For instance, consider we have a student database containing student records with their aggregate marks. If we wanted to allocate a scholarship to a student with marks above 90%, we would use a decision statement to determine if the marks are above 90% and then export that name.

The simplest form of a decision making statement is the 'if' statement. The basic structure of this is shown below.

```
If ( condition ) : //Execute code
```

In the above abstract code snippet, we can see that the code will be executed based on the outcome of the 'if' condition. Only when the condition is true, will the subsequent statements be executed. There are different types of decision making statements, and in this chapter we will go through each of them in more detail.

9.1 If Statement

The 'if' statement allows us to perform an action only if a certain condition evaluates to true. The general syntax of the 'if' statement is given below.

```
If ( condition ) : //Execute code
```

Let's now look at an example of how this loop can be used.

Example 34: The following program showcases the if statement.

```
# Decision making statements
a= 10
if ( a == 10 ) : print("The value of a is 10")
```

This program's output will be as follows:

The value of a is 10

In the above program:

- We are first defining a variable called 'a'.

- The variable holds a value of 10.

- Now we use the 'if' statement with a condition that checks whether 'a' is equal to 10.

- If 'a' is indeed equal to 10, we print the statement to the console 'The value of a is 10'.

9.2 If-Else Statement

The 'if-else' statement is similar to the 'if' statement, however it provides an additional option to execute another statement when the condition does not evaluate to true. The general syntax of the 'if-else' statement is given below.

```
if (condition) :

//Execute code

else:

//Execute code
```

Here with the help of the 'else' clause we have the ability to specify a code block, which can be executed if the condition evaluates to false. Let's look at an example of how this loop can be used.

Example 35: The following program shows how to use the if-else statement.

```
# Decision making statements
a= 11
if ( a == 10 ) : print("The value of a is 10")
else : print("The value of a is not equal to 10")
```

This program's output will be as follows:

The value of a is not equal to 10

In the above program:

- We are first defining a variable called 'a'.

- The variable holds a value of 11.

- Now we use the 'if' statement, which has a condition that checks if the value of 'a' is equal to 10. If it is, a statement will be printed to the console.

- We are also specifying an 'else' condition, which will print a different statement to the console if the value of 'a' does not equal 10.

- In this example, the 'else' condition will be executed.

9.3 Nested If-Else Statement

We can also nest 'if' statements inside of each other. For example, when the first 'if' condition evaluates to false, a second 'if' condition will be evaluated. An example of this structure is given below.

```
if condition1:

//Execute code

   elif condition2:

   //Execute code

else:

//Execute code
```

Let's look at an example of how this loop can be used.

Example 36: This program showcases a nested if-else statement.

```
# Decision making statements
a= 6
```

```
if ( a > 10 ) : print("The value of a is greater than 10")
elif (a > 5) : print("The value of a is greater than 5 and less than 10")
else : print("The value of a is not known")
```

This program's output will be as follows:

The value of a is greater than 5 and less than 10

In the above program:

- We are first defining a variable called 'a'.

- The variable holds a value of 6.

- We use the 'if' statement to check whether the value of 'a' is greater than 10. If it is, a statement will be printed to the console.

- In a situation where the 'if' statement is false, the following 'elif' statement will check whether the value of 'a' is greater than 5. If it is, a different statement will be printed to the console.

- Finally if both the 'if' and 'elif' statements are false, the 'else' statement will be executed.

- In our example, the 'elif' statement is executed.

10. Loops

Loops work similarly to decision making statements, except that they are used to iterate through a set of values. So if we again have a student database containing student records with their aggregate marks, we could use a loop statement to iterate through the entire database and extract all names with an aggregate mark above 90%.

There are different types of loop statements, and in this chapter we will go through each of them in more detail.

10.1 While Loops

The general syntax of the 'while' loop is given below

```
While (condition)

//Execute code
```

In this code, for as long as the condition we specify evaluates to true, the code statement will execute each time as it runs through the set of values. Let's look at an example of the 'while' statement.

Example 37: The following program shows how to use the while loop.

```python
# Using loops in python
count = 0
while (count < 5):
    print("The value of count is ", count)
    count = count + 1
```

This program's output will be as follows:

The value of count is 0

The value of count is 1

The value of count is 2

The value of count is 3

The value of count is 4

In the above program:

- We first define the value of a variable called 'count' to 0.

- We then use the 'while' loop.

- In the 'while' loop we are specifying the condition that a statement will be executes as long as 'count' equals less than 5.

- The code that will be executed prints a statement to the console.

- And then we increment the value of 'count' by 1.

- This program will loop until the value of 'count' equals 5.

10.2 For Loops

The general syntax of the 'for' loop is given below.

```
for variable in expression

//Execute code
```

In the 'for' clause, we specify a range or list that will be iterated through in sequence. Each time the program will assign the next item in the list to the variable we specify, and then execute the statement block. This process will continue until the range or list is exhausted. Let's look at an example of the 'for' loop statement.

Example 38: The next program showcases the for loop.

```
# Using loops in python
for x in range(0, 3):
    print("The value is ",x)
```

This program's output will be as follows:

The value is 0

The value is 1

The value is 2

In the above program:

- We are defining the 'for' loop statement.

- This statement consists of the keyword 'for', the variable 'x' and the range of '0 to 3'.

- This range can easily be replaced with a defined list.

61

- For each range value, it will be assigned to the variable 'x'.

- And will then be displayed to the console.

10.3 Break and Continue Statements

We can also use the 'break' and 'continue' statements in Python loops. The 'break' statement terminates and exits the current loop completely, while the 'continue' statement rejects the current iteration of the loop and continues to the next iteration while staying within the overall loop.

- break = exit loop

- continue = exit iteration

Let's look at an example of the 'break' statement.

Example 39: This program shows how to use a break statement in loops.

```
# Using loops in python
count = 0
while (count < 5):
    print("The value of count is ", count)
    count = count + 1
    if ( count > 3) : break
```

This program's output will be as follows:

The value of count is 0

The value of count is 1

The value of count is 2

The value of count is 3

In the above program:

- This time in the 'for' loop we are using the 'break' statement.

- The 'break' statement will reject the current iteration of the loop and exit the loop if its condition is met.

- This means that if the program encounters a value greater than 3, it will not print the value to the console, and will immediately exit the loop.

Now let's look at an example of the 'continue' statement.

Example 40: The following program shows how to use a continue statement in loops.

```
# Using loops in python
for x in range(10):

    if x % 2 == 0:
     continue
    print(x)
```

This program's output will be as follows:

1

3

5

7

9

In the above program:

- This time in the 'for' loop we are using the 'continue' statement.

- The 'continue' statement will reject the current iteration of the loop and move onto the next iteration of the loop, if its condition is met.

- This means that if the program encounters an even value, it will not print the value to the console, and will move onto the next value in the loop.

10.4 Nested Loops

We can also nest loops inside of other loops. So instead of executing a statement inside of a loop, an entirely different loop can be executed. This is best described by way of an example.

Example 41: The following program showcases nested loops.

```
# Using loops in python

i=0
while (i < 3):
    j=0
    while (j < 2):
        print("The value of j is ", j)
        j = j + 1
    print("The value of i is ", i)
    i = i + 1
```

This program's output will be as follows:

The value of j is 0

The value of j is 1

The value of i is 0

The value of j is 0

The value of j is 1

The value of i is 1

The value of j is 0

The value of j is 1

The value of i is 2

In the above program:

- We are using 2 'while' loops. A loop for variable 'j' inside a loop for variable 'i'.

- Each time the 'i' loop executes once, the 'j' loop will go through all of its iterations.

- It can be easy to get stuck in an unending loop when using nested loop statements, so care should be taken with their use.

11. Working with Numbers

We have briefly looked at numbers in the Data Types chapter. In this chapter we will go into greater detail on how to use and manipulate numbers in Python. Before we go any further, let's have a brief refresher on the different types of numbers available in Python.

- Integer - These are whole numbers without fractions or decimals.

- Floating Point - These are numbers that have fractional parts expressed with a decimal point.

- Complex - These are complex numbers expressed by using a 'J' or 'j' suffix.

Let's look at a quick example of how these number data types can be used.

Example 42: This program shows how to use number data types in Python.

```
# This program looks at number data types
# An int data type
a=123
# A float data type
b=2.23
# A complex data type
c=3.14J
print(a)
```

```
print(b)
print(c)
```

This program's output will be as follows:

123

2.23

3.14j

There are a variety of functions available in Python to work with numbers. Let's look at a summary of them, after which we will look at each in more detail along with a simple example.

Table 7: Number Functions

Function	Description
abs()	This returns the absolute value of a number
ceil()	This returns the ceiling value of a number
max()	This returns the largest value in a set of numbers
min()	This returns the smallest value in a set of numbers
pow(x,y)	This returns the power of x to y
sqrt()	This returns the square root of a number
random()	This returns a random value
randrange(start, stop,step)	This returns a random value from a particular range

Function	Description
sin(x)	This returns the sin value of a number
cos(x)	This returns the cosine value of a number
tan(x)	This returns the tangent value of a number

11.1 Abs Function

This function is used to return the absolute value of a number. Let's look at an example of this function.

Example 43: The following program showcases the abs function.

```
# This program looks at number functions
a=-1.23
print(abs(a))
```

This program's output will be as follows:

1.23

11.2 Ceil Function

This function is used to return the ceiling value of a number. Let's look at an example of this function. Note that for this program we need to import the 'math' module in order to use the 'ceil' function.

Example 44: The following program showcases the ceil function.

```
import math
# This program looks at number functions
a=1.23
print(math.ceil(a))
```

This program's output will be as follows:

2

11.3 Max Function

This function is used to return the largest value in a set of numbers. Let's look at an example of this function.

Example 45: The program below is used to showcase the max function.

```
# This program looks at number functions
print(max(3,4,5))
```

This program's output will be as follows:

5

11.4 Min Function

This function is used to return the smallest value in a set of numbers. Let's look at an example of this function.

Example 46: The following program shows how the min function works.

```
# This program looks at number functions
print(min(3,4,5))
```

This program's output will be as follows:

3

11.5 Pow Function

This function is used to return the value of x to the power of y, where the syntax is 'pow(x,y)'. Let's look at an example of this function.

Example 47: The following program showcases the pow function.

```
# This program looks at number functions
print(pow(2,3))
```

This program's output will be as follows:

8

11.6 Sqrt Function

This function is used to return the square root of a number. Let's look at an example of this function. Note that for this program we need to import the 'math' module in order to use the 'sqrt' function.

Example 48: The next program shows how the sqrt function works.

```
import math
# This program looks at number functions
print(math.sqrt(9))
```

This program's output will be as follows:

3.0

11.7 Random Function

This function is used to simply return a random value. Let's look at an example of this function.

Example 49: The following program showcases the random function.

```
import random
# This program looks at number functions
print(random.random())
```

The output will differ depending on the random number generated. Also note that for this program we need to use the 'random' Python library. In our case, the program's output is:

0.005460085356885691

11.8 Randrange Function

This function is used to return a random value from a particular range. Let's look at an example of this function.

Note that we again need to import the 'random' library for this function to work.

Example 50: This program is used to showcase the random function.

```
import random
# This program looks at number functions
print(random.randrange(1,10,2))
```

The output will differ depending on the random number generated. In our case, the program's output is:

5

11.9 Sin Function

This function is used to return the sine value of a number. Let's look at an example of this function.

Example 51: The following program shows how to use the sin function.

```
import math
# This program looks at number functions
print(math.sin(45))
```

This program's output will be as follows:

0.8509035245341184

11.10 Cos Function

This function is used to return the cosine value of a number. Let's look at an example of this function.

Example 52: This program is used to showcase the cos function.

```
import math
# This program looks at number functions
print(math.cos(45))
```

This program's output will be as follows:

0.5253219888177297

11.11 Tan Function

This function is used to return the tangent value of a number. Let's look at an example of this function.

Example 53: The following program shows the use of the tan function.

```
import math
# This program looks at number functions
print(math.tan(45))
```

This program's output will be as follows:

1.6197751905438615

12. Working with Strings

In an earlier section, we briefly covered the string data type. In this chapter we will look at strings in more detail. More specifically, we will cover the various string operators and string functions available in Python. Recall that a string is merely a series of text characters. Let's look at a simple example to refresh our memory.

Example 54: The following program showcases the string data type.

```
# This program looks at string functions
str="Hello World"
print(str)
```

This program's output will be as follows:

Hello World

12.1 String Operators

There are various operators that can be used to work with strings in Python. An operator is a symbol that performs a specific operation. In this instance, the operation is performed on strings. Let's look at the various string operators in more detail, along with a simple example for each.

12.1.1 Concatenation Operator (+)

This operator can be used to concatenate strings. Let's look at an example of this.

Example 55: The following program showcases the concatenation operator.

```
# This program looks at string functions
str1="Hello "
str2="World"
print(str1+str2)
```

This program's output will be as follows:

Hello World

12.1.2 Repetition Operator (*)

This operator creates multiple copies of a string. Let's look at an example of this.

Example 56: The following program showcases the repetition operator.

```
# This program looks at string functions
str1="Hello "
print(str1*3)
```

This program's output will be as follows:

Hello Hello Hello

12.1.3 Slice Operator ([x])

This operator will retrieve a specified character from a particular index in a string. In this syntax 'x' denotes the character position in the string, with zero being the first character. Let's look at an example of this.

String	H	e	l	l	o
Index	0	1	2	3	4

Example 57: The following program showcases the slice operator.

```
# This program looks at string functions
str1="Hello "
print(str1[1])
print(str1[2])
```

This program's output will be as follows:

e
l

12.1.4 Range Slice Operator ([x:y])

This operator will retrieve a specified range of characters from a particular index in a string. In this syntax 'x' denotes the first character (which will be included) and 'y' denotes the last character (which will be excluded) of the string to be retrieved. When referring to the target string, the first character will be zero.

String	H	e	l	l	o
Index	0	1	2	3	4

Example 58: This program shows how to use the range slice operator.

```
# This program looks at string functions
str1="Hello "
print(str1[1:3])
```

This program's output will be as follows:

el

12.1.5 In Operator (in)

This operator searches for a specified character in a target string. If the character exists in the string a value of 'True' is returned, else it returns 'False'. Let's look at an example of this.

Example 59: The program below showcases the 'in' operator.

```
# This program looks at string functions
str1="Hello "
print('e' in str1)
print('a' in str1)
```

This program's output will be as follows:

True

False

12.1.6 Not In Operator (not in)

This operator does the opposite of the 'in' operator. It searches for a specified character in a target string. But if the character does not exist in the string a value of 'True' is returned, else it returns 'False'. Let's look at an example of this.

Example 60: The following program showcases the 'not in' operator.

```
# This program looks at string functions
str1="Hello "
print('a' not in str1)
print('e' not in str1)
```

This program's output will be as follows:

True

False

12.2 String Functions

There are a variety of built-in functions available in Python to work with strings. A built-in function makes programming considerably easier by providing functionality, without the need to create it from scratch. Let's look at these functions in more detail.

Table 8: String Functions

Function	Description
capitalize()	This capitalizes the first letter of the string

Function	Description
center(width,char)	This returns a string that is at least the specified width, created by padding the string with the character
count(str)	This returns the number of times a string is contained in another string
find(str)	This returns the index number of the substring in a string
isalpha()	This checks if all characters of a string are alphabetic characters
isdigit()	This checks if a string contains only digits
islower()	This checks if a string contains all lower case characters
isupper()	This checks if a string contains all upper case characters
len()	This returns the length of the string
lower()	This returns the string in lower case
upper()	This returns the string in upper case
replace()	This replaces a string with a new string
split()	This splits a string based on the split character

12.2.1 Capitalize Function

This function is used to capitalize the first letter of a string. Let's look at an example of this function.

Example 61: The following program showcases the capitalize function.

```
# This program looks at string functions
str1="hello "
print(str1.capitalize())
```

This program's output will be as follows:

Hello

12.2.2 Center Function

This function returns a string that is centered in new string. Additional space is padded with a specified fill character. The syntax for this function is:

```
center(string width,fill character)
```

Let's look at an example of this function.

Example 62: The program below shows how to use the center function.

```
# This program looks at string functions
str1="hello"
print(str1.center(10,'1'))
```

This program's output will be as follows:

11hello111

12.2.3 Count Function

This function returns the number of times a string is contained in another string. Let's look at an example of this function.

Example 63: This program shows how to use the count function.

```
# This program looks at string functions
str1="Hello Hello World"
print(str1.count("Hello"))
```

This program's output will be as follows:

2

12.2.4 Find Function

This function searches for and returns the index number of a specified string in another string. It will return the first position of the first character of the specified string. Let's look at an example of this function.

Example 64: The following program showcases the find function.

```
# This program looks at string functions
str1="Hello Hello World"
print(str1.find("Hello"))
```

This program's output will be as follows:

0

12.2.5 Isalpha Function

This function checks whether all characters in a string are alphabetic characters only. It will return 'True' if they are, else it will return 'False'. Let's look at an example of this function.

Example 65: The program below showcases the isalpha function.

```
# This program looks at string functions
str1="Hello"
print(str1.isalpha())
```

This program's output will be as follows:

True

12.2.6 Isdigit Function

This function checks whether all characters in a string are digit characters only. It will return 'True' if they are, else it will return 'False'. Let's look at an example of this function.

Example 66: This program shows how the isdigit function works.

```
# This program looks at string functions
str1="1"
print(str1.isdigit())
```

This program's output will be as follows:

True

12.2.7 Islower Function

This function checks whether all letters in a string are lowercase. It will return 'True' if they are, else it will return 'False'. Let's look at an example of this function.

Example 67: The following program is used to showcase the islower function.

```
# This program looks at string functions
str1="hello"
print(str1.islower())
```

This program's output will be as follows:

True

12.2.8 Isupper Function

This function checks whether all letters in a string are uppercase. It will return 'True' if they are, else it will return 'False'. Let's look at an example of this function.

Example 68: The next program showcases the isupper function.

```
# This program looks at string functions
str1="HELLO"
print(str1.isupper())
```

This program's output will be as follows:

True

12.2.9 Len Function

This function returns the length of a string. Let's look at an example of this function.

Example 69: The following program shows how to use the len function.

```
# This program looks at string functions
str1="hello"
print(len(str1))
```

This program's output will be as follows:

5

12.2.10 Lower Function

This function returns the string in lowercase form. Let's look at an example of this function.

Example 70: The program below showcases the lower function.

```
# This program looks at string functions
str1="HELLO"
print(str1.lower())
```

This program's output will be as follows:

hello

12.2.11 Upper Function

This function returns the string in uppercase form. Let's now look at an example of this function.

Example 71: The following program shows how the upper function works.

```
# This program looks at string functions
str1="hello"
print(str1.upper())
```

This program's output will be as follows:

HELLO

12.2.12 Replace Function

This function replaces a specified string with a new string, in the original string. The syntax for this function is:

```
replace(old string,new string,number of replacements)
```

The number of replacements is optional, if we wished to limit how many strings are to be replaced. Let's now look at an example of this function.

Example 72: This program showcases the replace function.

```
# This program looks at string functions
str1="hello new"
print(str1.replace("new","world"))
```

This program's output will be as follows:

hello world

12.2.13 Split Function

This function splits a string based on a specified split character. It will then return a delimited list of strings. Let's look at an example of this function.

Example 73: The following program is used to showcase the split function.

```
# This program looks at string functions
str1="hello hello hello"
print(str1.split(" "))
```

This program's output will be as follows:

['hello', 'hello', 'hello']

13. Type Conversion

Sometimes there is a need to convert from one data type to another. We might want to convert from an integer to a floating point number or from a number to a string, depending on what the value will be used for. Python has the necessary functions to perform the job. Let's look at the functions available for this purpose.

Table 9: Type Conversion Functions

Function	Description
float()	This is used to convert a value to a floating point number
int()	This is used to convert a value to an integer number
str()	This is used to convert a value to its string representation
complex()	This is used to convert a value to its complex number representation
ord()	This is used to convert a character to its Unicode representation

13.1 Float Function

This function is used to convert a value to a floating point number. Recall that a floating point value is simply a decimal number. Let's look at an example of this function.

Example 74: The following program showcases the float function.

```
# This program looks at string functions
a=1
print(a)
print(float(a))
```

This program's output will be as follows:

1

1.0

13.2 Int Function

This function is used to convert a value to an integer number. An integer number is a whole number. The function will not round a decimal number, but simply drop the decimal value. Let's look at an example of this function.

Example 75: The following program shows how to use the int function.

```
# This program looks at string functions
a=1.5
print(a)
print(int(a))
```

This program's output will be as follows:

1.5

1

13.3 Str Function

This function is used to convert a value to a string representation. Let's look at an example of this function.

Example 76: The program below showcases the str function.

```
# This program looks at string functions
a=1.0
print(a)
print(str(a))
```

This program's output will be as follows

1.0

1.0

13.4 Complex Function

This function is used to convert a value to a complex number representation. Let's look at an example of this function.

Example 77: The following program shows how the complex function works.

```
# This program looks at string functions
a=1.0
```

```
print(a)
print(complex(a))
```

This program's output will be as follows:

1.0

(1+0j)

13.5 Ord Function

This function is used to convert a character to its Unicode value. Its inverse is the 'Chr' function, which returns the character based on the Unicode value. These are not commonly used, but do have their place in programming. Let's look at an example of this function.

Example 78: The program below showcases the chr function.

```
# This program looks at string functions
a="a"
print(a)
print(ord(a))
b=97
print(b)
print(chr(b))
```

This program's output will be as follows

a

97

97

a

92

Conclusion

You have made it to the end of the first book in our Step-By-Step Python series. If you enjoyed getting started with Python, there is so much more to learn and do with this wonderful language. Be sure to keep a lookout for upcoming books in this series.

Python is a valuable programming language with a large array of uses. It is practical, efficient, and extremely easy to use. It will be a great asset and reference point for your future in programming. If you can think it, you can create it. Don't be afraid to try something new.

Good luck and happy programming!

About the Author

Nathan Clark is an expert programmer with nearly 20 years of experience in the software industry.

With a master's degree from MIT, he has worked for some of the leading software companies in the United States and built up extensive knowledge of software design and development.

Nathan and his wife, Sarah, started their own development firm in 2009 to be able to take on more challenging and creative projects. Today they assist high-caliber clients from all over the world.

Nathan enjoys sharing his programming knowledge through his book series, developing innovative software solutions for their clients and watching classic sci-fi movies in his free time.